Birdoswald Roman Fort

Tony Wilmott

Introduction

For 300 years, from the 2nd to the 5th centuries, Birdoswald was one of 16 forts built as part of the Hadrian's Wall frontier system. Today, its defences are the best preserved of any along the Wall.

After the Romans left Britain, people continued to live on the site, so, as well as the Roman history, there are a further 1,000 years of human occupation to discover here. The excavation of wooden halls from the obscure period after the end of Roman Britain was one of the most important discoveries on the Wall in recent history, revealing for the first time life here during the so-called Dark Ages.

Birdoswald was then deserted for five centuries but reoccupied in the 11th century: medieval buildings within the sheltering Roman walls are still visible. By the 16th century, Birdoswald was a fortified farm subject to raids by reivers from Liddesdale, now in Scotland. The situation became more peaceful in the 18th century and interest in the history of the site began to grow. The first excavations took place in the mid-19th century, and have continued to the present. Until 1984 Birdoswald was still farmed and the site visitors see today, with its farmhouse and related buildings and excavated Roman and medieval remains, reflects the many layers of the settlement's past.

The site lies within a meander of the River Irthing and the view into the gorge was once compared to that from Troy. Also spectacular are the views south of the Irthing valley and Cold Fell and east towards the wave-like crags of the Great Whin Sill.

Above: Engraved gemstones from Roman rings found at Birdoswald from 1987. From top, glass intaglio of the minor god Bonus Eventus; jasper intaglio of a member of the Imperial family; jasper intaglio showing a pair of shrimps

Facing page: Birdoswald seen from the north-west

The Tour

Birdoswald is a complex site, spanning 1,800 years of history – including Romans, border raiders and Victorian romantics. The layers of history have presented archaeologists with a fascinating challenge. The old farmhouse and surrounding buildings stand on the site of the Roman fort and are all built out of reused Roman masonry.

USING THE TOUR

The tour begins outside the door of the shop. The excavated area of the fort is entered through the main west gate. The route follows the main street, then leads to the south gate and the viewpoint over the river. From the main east gate, two routes take the visitor either along Hadrian's Wall to the milecastle or back to the shop. Small numbered plans in the margins highlight key points on the tour of the excavated site.

THE COURTYARD AND EXHIBITION

The tour starts outside the shop in the rear courtyard of the former Birdoswald farm. The visitor centre is housed in farm buildings that date from the 18th and 19th centuries and were built in the sheltered north-west corner of the Roman fort.

Opposite the exhibition and to the right of the toilets, a large brown stone can be seen built into the wall of the modern building. This is a fragment of a Roman altar dedicated by the *cohors I Aelia Dacorum miliaria*, the garrison of the fort in the 3rd and 4th centuries. The stone is a reminder that all the farm buildings on the site are built out of Roman stone quarried from the fort's remains.

The building in which the exhibition is displayed has stone windows incorporating Roman arched window heads excavated at the main east gate of the fort in 1855. One exhibit to look out for here is the sculpture of Jupiter and Vulcan which, although now worn, would originally have been brightly painted. One of the most important finds from the site is also on display – an altar dedicated to the woodland deity Silvanus by the *Venatores Bannienses*, literally 'the hunters of Banna' (illustrated on page 26). This is the only object found within the fort of Birdoswald to record its Roman name of Banna.

 BARRACK BLOCKS

Now hidden under the floors of the farm buildings and courtyard are the remains of a pair of standard Roman infantry barrack blocks. The site was excavated during the refurbishment of the farm buildings to create the visitor centre. The barracks were long, narrow buildings divided into eight rooms of a similar size, *contubernia*. Each housed an infantry century (see page 33). At Birdoswald, each room would have been shared by 10 men.

At the western end of the barracks were larger blocks of apartments projecting slightly beyond the building frontage. Each block would have housed an infantry centurion and his household, with perhaps a subordinate officer and his family, too. Excellent examples of such buildings can be seen at Chesters Roman Fort.

The barracks were frequently altered to reflect changes in the garrison and in Roman army organisation. In the early 3rd century AD, the northernmost barrack was rebuilt with separate officers' quarters, equipped with a hypocaust, or underfloor heating system, a rare feature in Roman barracks. A broad veranda was added to the front of the soldiers' quarters. By the early 4th century, the barracks had been replaced by small, free-standing barrack rooms of a kind better seen at the fort at Housesteads. One officer's house included a room with an apse, possibly indicating a Christian chapel.

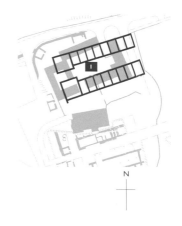

Top: Illustration of sculpture from Birdoswald of Vulcan (with pincers) and Jupiter (with hole for thunderbolt), as it might have once looked
Above: Altar built into the modern wall dedicated by the tribune Domitius Honoratus

Facing page: Detail of enamelled plate from a military belt, probably of Legion II Augusta, from the primary timber fort

5

RECONSTRUCTION OF THE EARLY 3RD-CENTURY FORT

The reconstruction has been compiled using information from excavations (E) or geophysics (G)

1 Main north gate, *porta principalis* (assumed) – now under road

2 Infantry barracks (E)

3 Drill and exercise hall (E)

4 Granaries (E)

5 Main west gate, *porta principalis sinistra* (E)

6 Fort ditches (E)

7 Headquarters building, *principia* (G)

8 Infantry barracks (E, G)

9 Store buildings/workshops (E)

Above: *Artist's impression of the fort and civilian settlement,*
as it may have looked in the early 3rd century

10 Commander's residence, *praetorium* (E, G)

11 Rear area of fort, *retentura* (G)

12 Main south gate, *porta decumana* (E)

13 Main east gate, *porta principalis dextra* (E)

14 Angle towers (E)

15 Interval towers (E)

16 Signal tower (E, G)

17 Civilian settlement, *vicus* (G)

18 Gateway over Vallum, or earthworks (E)

19 Hadrian's Wall (E)

2 MAIN WEST GATE

Follow the signs to the fort, past the door to the farmhouse, and down the path to the left. From the top of the bank, the main west gate, or *porta principalis sinistra* can be seen.

The main west gate is one of the four double gates on each side of the fort. Each had two arched entrances supported by six large stone piers and was flanked by two towers with guard-chambers on the ground floor. Above the arches was a second storey connecting the towers. It is probable that the wall-top was patrolled and the rooms over the gate were reached through doors at wall-top level. Above the gates was a crenellated platform flanked by the tiled-roof top storeys of the towers.

The gate was rebuilt in the early 3rd century. The extraordinarily high-quality stonework visible to the right of the gate is the most impressive masonry anywhere on Hadrian's Wall. It seems unlikely that it was dressed merely for the lower storey of a fort gate. At the far end of the block it is clear that it was inserted into the rest of the rougher stonework of the fort wall. It is probable that the masonry was originally part of another structure and it is tempting, in view of its quality, to suspect that it came from a major imperial monument, such as the base for an important statue, somewhere on the site.

In the middle of the 3rd century, the gate's southern, or right-hand, entrance was walled up. The causeway leading to the gate crosses the ditch, originally 2m (6ft) deep, which surrounded the fort. The top of a stone footbridge, built over the ditch in the 4th century, can be seen under the causeway to the right. In the centre of the entrance is a large stone block against which the inward-opening timber gates closed. They swung on wooden posts, protected at top and bottom with iron shoes. The bottom socket in which the gates turned survives. In front of the blocked entrance to the right is a continuous stone sill which was the original gate-stop. One of

Top: Artist's impression of the main west gate in the mid-3rd century, showing the southern entrance being walled up
Above: *Pottery plaque from Corbridge, showing a Roman blacksmith: the walled-up southern gate became a smithy in the 3rd century*

the sockets has an iron pivot. During the 3rd century the guard-chambers and the area inside the blocked gate were used for ironworking and the circular area of stone flagging in the north guard-chamber was the base for a smithy. The gate survived as the site's main entrance until the 14th century.

The area inside the gate was excavated between 1987 and 1992. This revealed important evidence for the Roman occupation from the early 2nd century to a period beyond the date usually accepted date for the end of Roman Britain in the early 5th century. Although uninhabited from then until the 13th century, the site has been occupied ever since and has been laid out to show several phases in its history.

3 FARMHOUSE AND MAIN STREET

Standing inside the west gate, the visitor looks straight down the main street of the fort, the *via principalis*. To left and right, a road ran around the inside of the fort walls (the intervallum road). The most obvious structure is the farmhouse, which now provides accommodation for visitors. The earliest section of the farmhouse to the east of the porch dates from the late 17th century. The central part, excluding the tower and porch, was built in the mid-18th century by Anthony and Margaret Bowman, commemorated by the inscription 'AMB 1745' inside the house. In 1858, Birdoswald's then owner, Henry Norman added a tower and porch, giving the house its current form. His initials, with the date, can be seen above the porch. Norman also laid out a formal garden which occupied the excavated area, and had the east and south gates of the fort excavated (see page 18).

Below: Plan of the farmhouse, showing the stages of its construction
Bottom: The farmhouse, with the excavated site in the foreground

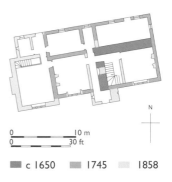

| 0 | 10 m |
| 0 | 30 ft |

■ c 1650   ■ 1745   ■ 1858

Top: Drawing of how the granaries would have looked in the early 3rd century
Below: *A reconstruction of a section of sandstone granary roof, using Roman slates*

GRANARIES

The remains of the two granary buildings, or *horrea*, are on the right of the main fort road. An inscription found in 1929 suggests that they were completed in AD 205–208.

The granaries had thick stone walls to provide dry, cool, rodent-proof storage for perishable goods. The soldiers' staple diet was based on grain for bread and porridge. They ate meat and we can assume that they also consumed fruit and vegetables. The only archaeological evidence for the diet of the Birdoswald garrison comes from excavated animal bones and burnt grain. They stored wheat and also barley which suggests that beer was brewed. Many cattle shoulder bones were found and there is evidence that the soldiers ate pork, mutton, poultry and venison. Meat was preserved by smoking, drying or salting.

The granaries were probably two storeys high, with buttresses on the south sides. To prevent damp, they had raised floors and slots in the walls so that cool air could circulate to keep the grain fresh. The south granary is the best preserved. The south wall survives to a height of 2m (6ft) and the buttresses and underfloor slots can be seen clearly from the field. The small square holes near the top of the wall held timber scaffolding while the granary was being built. At each end of the building are broad entrances, originally raised above the level of the adjacent road and used as loading bays. The two buttresses flanking the entrances would have supported an extension of the roof, so that loading could take place under cover – essential in bad weather. In the flagstone thresholds are the sockets for the door pivots.

4 SOUTH GRANARY

At the east end of the south granary is a low, blocked door.
This would have allowed dogs to go under the granary floor
to hunt down rodents. The roofs were covered with
diamond-shaped sandstone slates and weighed more than
50 tonnes. One of the threshold stones at the east end is a
replica of an ornamental screen which had been
reused in this position. The original is in the exhibition. The
door at the western end was an alteration to the original
plan but again the sockets for the door pivots are visible.

In the mid-4th century, the south granary was adapted for
another use. We know this because the raised flagstone floor
was lifted and the ventilation space was filled with soil and
rubble. The floor was then replaced.

It is not known what the building was adapted for. At some
point a pair of stone hearths was built at the west end. Some
high-quality objects were found dropped in the debris around
the hearths, including a 4th-century gold earring, a jet ring and
a silver coin from the reign of Theodosius (AD 388–395), the
latest coin found on the site. After excavation, the surviving
flagstones of the 4th-century floor were relaid; the rest of this
floor is now represented by yellow gravel.

5 NORTH GRANARY

Nearest the main street lies the north granary, with much of
the Roman layout now exposed. The exterior walls can be
seen, as can the parallel walls which supported the flagstone
floor, a small part of which still occupies the south-east corner.
The south wall is well preserved: the buttresses and ventilation

Left: View of the south granary from
the 'intervallum' road, with part
of the north granary along side,
during excavation in 1988

Sleeper walls to support raised
granary floor

Buttressed south wall of the
south-granary building

Buttressed
south wall
of the north
granary
building

Broad doorway at
west end of granary.
Holes in the
threshold held the
pivots for the doors

slots are all visible. On the end of the fourth buttress from the east end, a fragment of an inscription, with the name IVLIVS ('Julius'), has been reused upside down.

The story of the north granary is very different to that of the south. At some point the roof collapsed, spreading broken slates into the alley between the granaries and across the floor of the building. A coin dated to AD 353 found beneath this debris proves that the collapse took place after this date. No effort was made to clear up or to reuse the building. It seems to have been left roofless and used as a convenient quarry for materials to repair other buildings.

6 TIMBER BUILDINGS

Probably after the south granary eventually collapsed, a timber building was built on the site of the north granary. First the floor was levelled by reusing building stones, then a new flagstone floor was laid. Shallow holes were cut in the low surviving walls to house structural posts and a building slightly longer than the former granary was erected. Apart from the holes left by the posts, there is no evidence of the materials used. It is likely that the roof was thatched. It must have been built after AD 395, the date of the latest coin found under it. It is impossible to know how long this building survived.

But this is not the end of the story. A second, even larger timber building (23m x 8.6m, or 75ft 6in x 28ft 3in) was built partly over the old north granary and partly over the main street. Its main timbers were pairs of posts (now represented by the paired timber uprights). The floor area over the main street is now represented by a rectangle of yellow gravel. It

Top: How the last timber building on the site of the north granary in the 5th century AD may have looked

Above: Gold earring found by a hearth in the reused south granary

lay further north, so that its north wall lined up with the spine of the west gate. (Looking down the northern row of timbers, this is very clear.) This large timber building would have been the first thing seen by anyone coming in through the gate.

⑦ SMALLER TIMBER BUILDINGS
Two smaller wooden buildings were built at the same time on the intervallum road to the west of the granaries. Their floor areas are also laid out in yellow gravel and the walls represented by timbers. They were built with beams laid on the ground into which upright posts were jointed.

A DARK AGE HALL
What might these timber buildings mean? There are a number of clues. They are a sequence – one replaced another. The reused south granary fell out of use to be replaced by the two successive phases of timber building. The best evidence for the function of these buildings comes from the site of the south granary, where the finds suggest the presence of high-ranking people occupying the space nearest the hearths. The second timber building was put in an obvious position in relation to the gate. This, with its size, suggests that it was important. The only similar buildings of this period to have been found are thought to be the timber halls of the warrior aristocracy of the so-called Dark Ages. Literature of the period is full of accounts of princely halls in which the war leader and his band would feast and entertain, as in the Anglo-Saxon poem *Beowulf* where the chieftain Hrothgar has 'the greatest of halls' where he 'hands out rings and treasure at the feast'. The hall was probably surrounded by smaller buildings for servants and retainers. We can visualise a community occupying a fortified place and led by a war leader from his great wooden hall. The old west gate was the entrance to his compound. There is no break in occupation, so this community must have developed from the Roman garrison.

Left: Excavation of the Dark Age Hall in 1987, its area marked in red, with archaeologists standing in the positions of the original timber posts

Above: Reconstruction drawing of the drill hall showing auxiliary infantry practising combat with wicker shields and wooden swords – such halls were essential for soldiers to have 'unceasing drill in wet and windy weather', according to the Roman writer Vegetius

Below: Carved graffito of a stallion at the foot of the south wall of the drill hall (facing the farmhouse tower)

8 DRILL HALL

Cross back to the northern side of the main street. Parts of two Roman buildings can be seen here. Running along the frontage of the street is a long, narrow building, first used as a storehouse but later as workshops, or *fabricae*. Behind it lay a drill hall, *basilica exercitatoria*, measuring 16m × 42.7m (52ft 6in × 140ft). The roof was supported by a double arcade based on a series of piers or columns flanking a broad nave. Light came from high windows above the arcade.

Roman military writers stressed the importance of weapons drill and exercise. At Birdoswald an indoor facility would have been essential. The basilica remained unaltered during the entire Roman period, a fact that shows its importance. About half of it now lies under the farmhouse, although the south-west corner can be seen in front of the farmhouse tower.

9 MEDIEVAL TOWER HOUSE

Around the south-west corner of the store/workshop is an L-shape of large, roughly dressed stones. This is all that remains of a medieval tower house, probably built between 1200 and 1500 in response to trouble on the border. There is no doubt that the Roman west gate was still in use at this time – more than 1,000 years after it was built – because medieval pottery was found under the collapsed stonework.

10 BASTLE HOUSE

After the gate collapsed, a bastle house – a defensible farmhouse typical of the Anglo-Scottish border during the late 16th century – replaced the tower house. The foundations of this building lie to the east of the farmhouse porch and are represented by stones laid on edge. The ground floor housed cattle while the family lived on the upper floor, reached by a ladder. This would have been pulled up in times of trouble. The only weak point was the doorway in the west end wall: the burning of doors, as happened at Birdoswald in 1590 (see page 36), was a favourite way of breaking and entering.

Above left: A typical bastle house at Black Middens, Northumberland, suggesting how Birdoswald may have looked in the 16th century
Left: Vicar's pele tower at Corbridge – the medieval tower house at Birdoswald was a similar size

Excavation and Discovery

The story of the main west gate at Birdoswald was crucial in understanding the history of the site. In this photograph the whole of its history is visible in cross-section

As sites are used they are changed by all kinds of human activity. Most actions, such as building, digging pits and so on, leave traces in the ground which archaeologists disentangle and interpret. Sites occupied for long periods, such as Birdoswald, are highly complex, as earlier evidence becomes disturbed. Archaeologists remove the latest deposit or structure first so that the site is excavated in the reverse order to that in which it was built up. As each layer is removed it is destroyed and so careful and accurate records need to be kept. Each layer may contain objects from the past. Some, such as pottery and coins, help to date a site, while others provide evidence for other aspects of daily life. Soil samples may yield microscopic pollen grains, carbonised seeds, tiny bones or insect remains which indicate the natural environment, crops grown or stored, and diet. Larger animal bones provide data on both animal husbandry and diet.

SECTION OF THE SOUTH ENTRANCE OF THE MAIN WEST GATE

1 The earlist evidence – the levelled remains of the Hadrianic Turf Wall

2 The stone foundations of the gate were cut into the original wall

3 The piers supporting the arches of the gate were begun

4 A layer of black soil over the foundations and against the piers shows that work halted

5 Gravel roads were laid above the black soil

6 By the early 3rd century the ground level had risen to hide the bottom two courses of the fort wall

7 The south gate tower was rebuilt with extraordinarily high-quality masonry, in the early 3rd century

8 The south gate entrance was walled up in the mid-3rd century

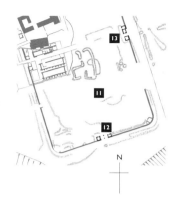

Ⅻ HEADQUARTERS

Continue along the line of the main Roman street, leaving the excavated area, and pass through the wooden gates in the screen of trees. In the Roman period this whole field was part of the fort and covered in buildings Straight ahead are the ruins of the main east gate. To the right, at the base of the ramp, are a series of earthworks. Turn right and walk through them. These mark the site of the headquarters building, or *principia*. This was the heart of the fort: the affairs of the regiment were administered and the official religion of the unit and the imperial cult was practised here. Excellent excavated examples of this kind of building can be seen on Hadrian's Wall at Housesteads, Vindolanda and Chesters. Now walk uphill along the mown path. This runs along the line of an excavation trench dug in 1931 across the back wall, showing that this survived to a height of 3m (9.8ft) from Roman ground level. Looking ahead, uphill, to the south gate, it is puzzling to realise that this, too, is at Roman ground level. The explanation lies in the natural topography of the site. The fort is built in a fold in the ground and across two ridges. One of these is marked by the main street, the other by the south gate. From the low point between these ridges, where you are now standing, the buildings of the fort were terraced uphill in both directions. The dip in the centre has become filled with demolition debris and soil, and as a result the buried buildings are in a good state of preservation. The depth of soil allowed the site to be ploughed in the Middle Ages: in a raking light, the east–west ridges and furrows of the medieval field system can be seen clearly.

Ⅻ SOUTH GATE

The south gate, *via decumana*, was excavated in 1852. Its plan is identical to that of the main west gate. Leaving the fort through this gate, bear right up to the ridge top close to the south-west corner. The view into the wooded gorge of the River Irthing was compared by a 19th-century Earl of Carlisle to that from Troy. It is worth pausing here; deer often run across the tongue of land on the far side of the river. A stone-lined prehistoric burial chamber was discovered here during excavations. Looking across the gorge to the wooded cliff edge to the right, you see the site of the Roman cemetery. Between the fort and the cemetery, and also on the east side of the fort, was an extensive civilian settlement, *vicus*. Nothing is visible of this settlement, which is known only from the evidence of geophysical survey.

ⅩⅢ MAIN EAST GATE

Return to the south gate and continue along the outside of the fort wall, round the south-east corner, and down the east side. The fort wall here shows several types of stonework,

Above: Gilt-bronze statue of Hercules, possibly intended as a likeness of the Emperor Commodus, found at Birdoswald in the 19th century

Right: View over the River Irthing
from the south of the fort
Below: Engraving by John Storey of
the main east gate, the best
preserved on Hadrian's Wall, when
it was first exposed in 1852.
The arched window heads, now in
the exhibition, are in the foreground

reflecting three centuries of repair and rebuilding. Between the corner and the main east gate is an area of collapsed wall, next to an opening in the wall which is the site of one of the two single-arched minor gates, *porta quintana dextra.* These were blocked early in the fort's history and remained a point of weakness. The angle at which the wall lies vividly recalls its final collapse.

Further down is the main east gate, *porta principalis dextra.* Excavated in 1852, this is the best preserved fort gate on Hadrian's Wall. There are two arched gateways, supported by piers built of large stone blocks. A single arch stone (voussoir) remains in place on the north-east pier. On each side is a guard-chamber with a doorway at the rear (the northern guard-chamber door was walled up in the 3rd century). The arched window-heads that can be seen in the exhibition were found here.

Death and Burial at Birdoswald

The evidence for death and burial ritual from the Wall is generally poor. Cemeteries, though known, have mostly not been excavated. At Birdoswald, the cemetery was discovered in 1961, when ploughing showed patches of burnt material, and turned up several complete pots, one of which contained ash and cremated bone. A number of tombstones have been found in and around Birdoswald, but only four have inscriptions. One of these is the memorial of Aurelius Concordius, the infant son of Aurelius Julianus, the commander of the Dacian cohort who had the fort granaries built (illustrated on page 26); another is the stone to the children Decebalus and Blaesus. The other two are soldiers: Septimus, who died at the age of 40 after serving in cohors I Aelia Dacorum for 18 years, and G. Cossurtius Saturninus, who was a soldier of Legion VI Victrix.

In 1999, the only complete burial assemblage ever excavated on Hadrian's Wall was recovered by Channel 4's Time Team at Birdoswald. A simple, large, black-burnished cooking pot contained the cremated bone. Buried with it was a small drinking cup made in Gaul. Both were 3rd century. The corpse had been burnt on a pyre, and the ashes then gathered together and placed in the urn. The small cup would have contained wine, either as a funerary drink for the mourners or to accompany the dead to the afterlife, or possibly scented oil to add to the pyre.

When the cremation urn was excavated in the laboratory, it was found to contain not only human bone but plaques of carved animal bone. These were probably attached either to a prized wooden casket that was burned on the pyre, or to a wooden bier on which the body lay.

Top: Excavation of a cremation at Birdoswald. The ashes were contained in an ordinary cooking pot (above), and a cup (centre) contained an offering of wine or oil. The bier was probably decorated with painted bone plaques
Left: Tombstone of G. Cossurtius Saturninus, of Legion VI Victrix. He was born in Hippo Regia, North Africa

Top: Stone statue of the seated goddess Fortuna, found in the bath-house of the commanding officer's house in 1855
Above: *A phallus, carved on the Wall, considered to be a good-luck symbol*

WALK 1: HADRIAN'S WALL TO HARROW'S SCAR MILECASTLE

There are now two choices of route. To reach the milecastle – one of 79 small garrisons placed at mile intervals along the wall – go through the kissing gate opposite the main east gate and walk downhill to Hadrian's Wall. Along this part of the Wall are a number of features. Near the drain running through the Wall at the fort end, an X is inscribed on a stone – probably a mason's mark. Above this X is a phallus, thought to avert the evil eye. Further along are three inscriptions, one a building stone of the eighth cohort, century of Julius Primus (COH VIII >IVL PRIMI) and one other phallic symbol. The locations of these features are marked with small metal strips. At the end of this stretch of wall is milecastle 49 (Harrow's Scar). This is not the best preserved of milecastles, but its basic plan – a rectangular fortlet attached to the Wall, but with rounded southern corners – is clear, as are the sites of the two large gates to north and south. The traces of internal buildings are the foundations of a 16th-century bastle house. From the point where the Wall has fallen into the river valley, the Roman bridge abutment at Willowford can be seen. This is reached by going down the steep path to the right, turning along the path to the left and crossing the footbridge (part of the Hadrian's Wall National Trail).

WALK 2: ALONG THE MAIN STREET

Go through the east gate back into the fort and along the main street. To the left, before the earthworks of the headquarters building, or *principia*, lay the commander's house, or *praetorium*. This Mediterranean-style courtyard house accommodated his household in some style. It had a private baths, where a statue of the goddess Fortuna was found in 1855. To the right of the street, a narrow store building occupied the street frontage, with barracks running back to the north wall of the fort, now under the road. The store building and the southern barrack were excavated in 1929.

NORTH WALL

To explore the north wall, return through the excavated area to the main west gate. From here the fort wall ran northwards, past the entrance to the farmyard. The fort wall has been robbed away, isolating three walls of an attached interval tower. The partially blocked doorway from the interior of the fort can be seen.

At the north corner of the fort, the lower storey of an angle tower can be seen. The door from the fort to this tower was blocked in the 3rd century, after it had been used as a bakehouse (the stone ovens survive well). Interval and angle towers were simple watchtowers, probably much like those which flanked the main gates. In the valley opposite the

Milecastle 49, Harrow's Scar | River Irthing | Modern footbridge | Roman bridge abutment at Willowford

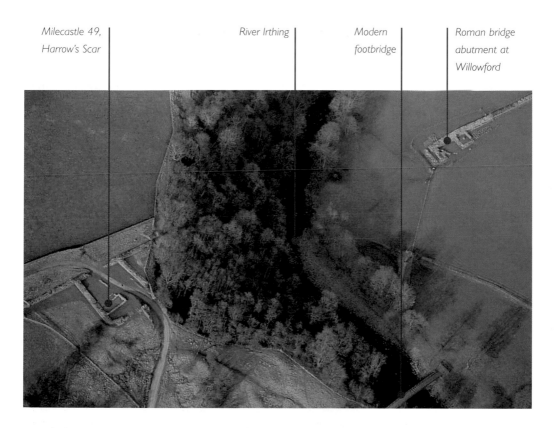

Above: Aerial view of the Roman crossing of the Irthing – erosion and deposition have greatly changed the river course here, as shown by the site of the Roman bridge

Left: Late-Roman tower on the eastern side of the river at Willowford bridge

north-west corner, seen in the middle distance, is the tower of the medieval castle of Triermain: Birdoswald was part of the lordship of Triermain throughout the Middle Ages. Visible on the horizon on a clear day is the flat-topped hill of Burnswark across the Solway in southern Scotland. On each side of it are Roman siege camps and nearby is the Hadrian's Wall outpost fort of Birrens. To the north, on the first ridge, at the edge of the plantation, is the line of the Maiden Way (see page 24).

To the right, along the fort's north wall, was a further interval tower. This was demolished and replaced in the early 3rd century AD by a bakehouse. In the two ovens here, modern red-coloured mortar represents the red burnt clay with which the stonework was originally bonded.

History

The history of
Birdoswald spans
that of Roman Hadrian's
Wall, the timber halls
of Dark Age chieftains,
and the turbulence
of medieval life along
the border.
Victorian romantic
taste influenced
the appearance of the
site. Its history has
been studied for more
than 400 years, since
the visit in 1599 of the
intrepid schoolmaster
Reginald Bainbrigg.

READING THE HISTORY

*This section describes the history of
Birdoswald up to the present. It
contains plans of the building of the
wall (pages 25–30), a section on
Birdoswald's Romanian connection
(page 32) and a feature on the
Roman army (page 33).*

HADRIAN'S WALL

After they invaded in AD 43, the Romans gradually conquered Britain – the governor Agricola finally defeating the Caledonians at the battle of Mons Graupius, near Inverness in AD 84. They built a network of roads and forts to control their new territory. In AD 87, a crisis on the Danube frontier led to the withdrawal of troops from Britain; by AD 100 the frontier had fallen back to the Tyne-Solway line. The frontier garrisons were stationed in forts (the best-known are Carlisle, Corbridge and Vindolanda) linked by a road, now known as the Stanegate. The reign of Hadrian (AD 117–138), however, marked a change in policy. Rather than extend the Empire, Hadrian wished to consolidate Roman territory behind secure frontiers. Part of this policy was the construction of his famous wall in Britain.

The Wall was begun in AD 122. It was a complex undertaking and the builders constantly changed their plans. In the original scheme there was a stone wall from Newcastle-upon-Tyne in the east to the River Irthing, with a barrier built of turf stretching from the Irthing to Bowness-on-Solway. At intervals of one Roman mile were small fortlets or milecastles which were defended gateways through the Wall, with two observation turrets in between. The milecastles in the stone Wall and all the turrets were built of stone, but milecastles on the Turf Wall were made of turf and timber. A ditch was dug on the north side of the Wall (except where the terrain made this unnecessary). Bridges were built over the north Tyne at Chesters and the

Above: Bronze portrait head of the Emperor Hadrian, found in the River Thames.
Below: Sequence of construction of Hadrian's Wall around Birdoswald

Facing page: Hadrian's Wall near Cawfields milecastle, showing the Wall on the crest of the ridge (left), with the great earthwork of the Vallum in the low land to the south (right)

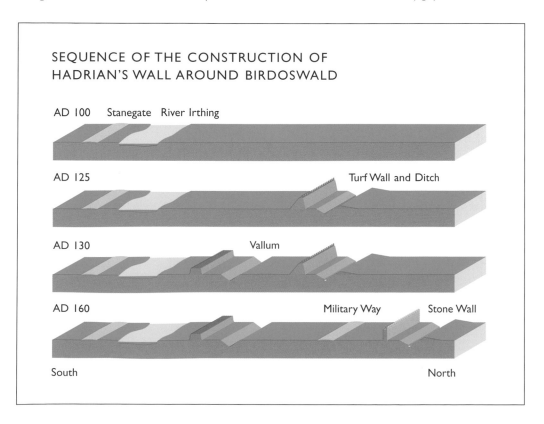

SEQUENCE OF THE CONSTRUCTION OF HADRIAN'S WALL AROUND BIRDOSWALD

AD 100   Stanegate   River Irthing

AD 125   Turf Wall and Ditch

AD 130   Vallum

AD 160   Military Way   Stone Wall

South   North

Above: Engraved gemstone carved with the imperial eagle and two military standards, from an iron ring found beneath the Turf Wall and dropped by one of its legionary builders
Below: Reconstruction of a leather tent – the first Roman tent leather fragments ever identified were found at Birdoswald in the 1930s

Irthing at Willowford. Garrison forts were sited on the line during the Wall's construction. Birdoswald is one of 15 such forts and was intended to guard the Irthing crossing. Originally timber, it was replaced in stone before AD 138.

To the north of the Wall was a series of outpost forts, probably used as bases for patrolling the territory of allied tribes. A road, called the Maiden Way, ran from the north gate of Birdoswald to the outpost fort of Bewcastle. The Vallum, a vast earthwork to the south of the Wall, was added during construction. This consisted of a flat-bottomed ditch 6m deep × 3m wide (19.7ft × 9.8ft), flanked by one of two banks set back 9m (29.5ft), each 6m (19.7ft) wide. This earthwork could be crossed only at monumental gates at the forts. Its function is not clearly understood.

2ND CENTURY

Shortly after the death of Hadrian, his successor, Antoninus Pius (AD 138–161), abandoned Hadrian's Wall as the frontier and moved the army northwards, building the Antonine Wall between the Forth and the Clyde. This was only half the length of Hadrian's Wall, though it had more forts and was built entirely of turf. It was occupied for just over 20 years and deserted in about AD 163 in favour of a return to Hadrian's Wall. Birdoswald may have remained in use at this time, as pottery and coins from the period have been found and the fort seems to have been maintained.

For the rest of the 2nd century, the frontier was a troubled place and its history is difficult to piece together. There is

Building the Wall

BEFORE THE ROMANS

At Birdoswald the Romans would have found a natural landscape consisting of dense woodland around a small basin mire – a bog. The trees on the site were mostly alder, with birch, oak and hazel. The evidence for this comes from pollen grains found beneath the Turf Wall.

more evidence from the reign of Emperor Septimius Severus (AD 193–211), when his governors carried out major refurbishment of Hadrian's Wall; their names occur repeatedly on building inscriptions. Birdoswald was refitted to accommodate a new auxiliary unit. The granaries were built in AD 205 to 208 under the governor Alfenus Senecio and the barrack blocks rebuilt and modified. At the same time, the interval tower on the north wall was turned into a bakehouse and the main east and west gates were both either repaired or rebuilt.

Above: Nessfield Wood, Shropshire – the mixture of species here is identical to the pollen record from pre-Roman Birdoswald, showing the kind of landscape the Romans encountered

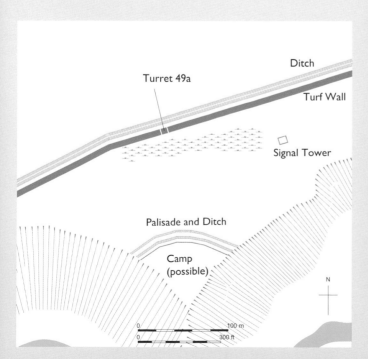

PHASE 1 AD 100–120

During the early 2nd century, from AD 100 to 120, a small, square tower was built at Birdoswald for signalling to the Stanegate frontier south of the river. The woodland was cleared and the Turf Wall constructed with free-standing stone towers. The builders of the Turf Wall may have set up camp behind the palisades and ditch, near the cliff edge (scraps of Roman tent leather were found in this area).

Above: 'The altar dedicated to Silvanus by the Venatores Bannienses' ('Deo Sancto Silvano Venatores Banniess'), the only inscription to show the fort's Roman name – Banna – and probably dating from the 3rd century

3RD CENTURY

In the 3rd century, the stones of Birdoswald suddenly speak: a large number of inscriptions of the period have been found. Several show that refurbishment continued for the first third of the 3rd century. The most important are the granary inscription (see page 10) and the stone from the main east gate recording building in AD 219. Both carry the badge and name of the new garrison which remained until the late 4th century, the *cohors I Aelia Dacorum miliaria*, an infantry regiment 1,000-strong which had originally been raised in Dacia, modern Romania. The unit is recorded on a large number of altars dedicated to *Iupiter Optimus Maximus*, 'Jupiter Best and Greatest', by a succession of commanding officers or tribunes. The inscriptions give the names of 17 such men. One of the earliest known is Aurelius Julianus, who is recorded on the granary-building inscription. In addition to the tribunes, the unit was commanded at times by legionary centurions and also a former member of the Praetorian Guard, Flavius Maximianus, who served during the 230s.

The 3rd century seems to have been peaceful on the northern frontier. Garrisons were static, with the same units based at their forts throughout the century. The civilian settlements, or *vici*, around the walls seem to have flourished. Examination in 1999 revealed that the settlement contained stone buildings with industrial and domestic functions (see page 30).

In AD 286, Carausius declared himself emperor of the British provinces. Saxon raiding ships started to appear in

PHASE 2 About AD 125
During the construction of the Wall, it was decided to build forts along it. These were originally planned to lie south of the Wall but this arrangement was later changed. We know little of the first fort at Birdoswald. It was built of turf and timber and projected to the north of the Wall. Its size is not certain. During the building of the forts, a huge earthwork, the Vallum, was built to the south of the Wall. It could be crossed only at the forts, through gateways.

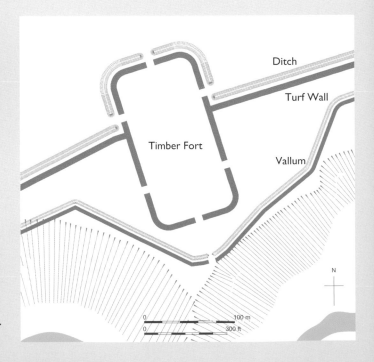

Ditch

Turf Wall

Timber Fort

Vallum

N

100 m
300 ft

the North Sea and English Channel. Carausius established a new frontier against them, known as the Saxon Shore, defended with forts on the south and east coasts. Some Wall forts may have been partly deserted to man the Shore forts. An inscription from between AD 297 and 305 records that the commander's residence was rebuilt, having 'fallen into ruin and become covered in earth'. The fort was probably abandoned for fewer than 29 years (AD 276–305).

Constantius Chlorus recovered the British provinces for Rome in AD 296. He campaigned against the Picts before his death in AD 306, as did his son, later known as Constantine the Great, in AD 312 and 314. Constantine the Great's troops first proclaimed him emperor at York, though it took him 20 years to become sole ruler of the empire.

Left: Scene of fort building from Trajan's Column in Rome (AD 113)

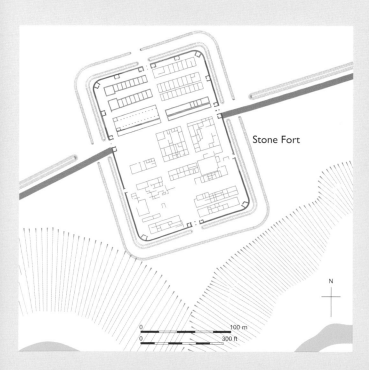

Stone Fort

PHASE 3 About AD 130–138 The Vallum was maintained along most of the Wall but at Birdoswald the ditch to the north of it was filled so that a bigger stone fort could be built. This fort, with its complex of streets and buildings, including drill hall, stores and barracks, was constructed quickly. The granaries, though, had not been built before the garrison was moved north by Antoninus Pius to refortify Scotland in the late 130s.

4TH CENTURY

The North was troubled during the 4th century. In AD 342, Constantine's son, the emperor Constans, was forced to come to Britain in the middle of winter to deal with unrest. In AD 360, Picts and Scots (a tribe from Ireland) attacked, and an army under a general Lupicinus was sent to suppress them. All this culminated in the so-called 'barbarian conspiracy' of AD 367, when several tribes invaded the province, killing two senior generals. Count Theodosius quelled the invasion and repaired the defences of the province. In AD 382, the usurper Magnus Maximus fought the Picts and Scots before his unsuccessful bid for the imperial throne. No signs of burning, looting or slaughter from this time exist on the Wall. The barbarians may have attacked by sea and then sailed round the frontier seeking richer, softer targets further south.

In the 4th century, the status and numbers of the frontier troops, known as *limitanei*, was reduced. At some forts, the long barrack blocks were replaced by rows of eight or nine individual buildings which held smaller numbers of soldiers. These are best seen at Housesteads.

At Birdoswald in the early 4th century, much renovation work was done. We know from the inscription mentioned above that the commander's residence was rebuilt and both the headquarters and fort baths were repaired. Archaeology shows that the western workshop was also rebuilt over the ruins of its predecessor. In the mid-4th century, the north granary collapsed and was quarried for building stone, while the southern granary was refurbished but no longer

Above: Enamelled bronze disc-brooch found at Birdoswald

PHASE 4 About AD 138
Just before Antoninus Pius's advance into Scotland, the Turf Wall was replaced in stone at Birdoswald. The new Wall followed a different course, abutting the north corners of the fort. The fort itself was now contained behind the Wall and no longer projected north of it. This stretch of the Wall, between Milecastle 49 at Harrow's Scar and Milecastle 51, is the only place where the stone rebuild did not follow the line of the Turf Wall exactly.

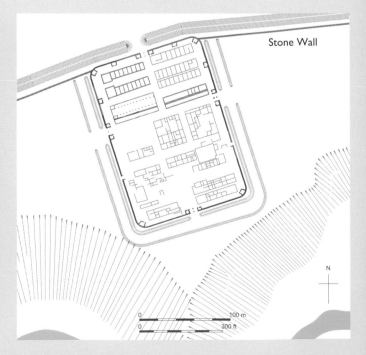

Stone Wall

0 100 m
0 300 ft

N

used for its original function. The fort may have been supplied with small amounts of grain by local farming settlements, and no longer needed large storage facilities.

LIFE ON THE WALL

The fort is not the whole of the story of Birdoswald. To west and east along the ridge stretched a civilian settlement. Because it has never been excavated there is little evidence of its date and an understanding of the activities that took place there can only be explored through parallels with other sites, particularly Vindolanda and Housesteads, where settlements have been excavated.

The geophysical survey of the civilian settlement has revealed mostly small, rectangular buildings. These are known as strip-houses, and would have had commercial premises in the front and domestic accommodation to the rear. On the west side of the fort, the survey seems to show an orderly layout of such buildings around an elliptical open space, almost like a medieval village green. To the east, the layout is less regular and includes at least one larger building which might have been a mansion or an inn for travellers – a similar building has been excavated at Vindolanda. Limited excavation has shown that the buildings had stone foundations and that they seem to have housed both domestic and small-scale industrial activities. The settlement was directly related to the fort and may have been administered by the commander or his deputies. The 2nd-century settlement housed the unofficial families of the troops, their slaves and servants, and, in the 3rd

Below: Roman leather shoe – a great many were preserved in the waterlogged conditions of the fort ditch

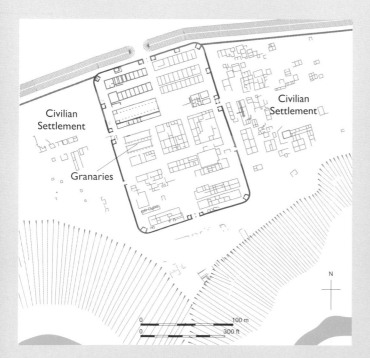

Civilian Settlement

Civilian Settlement

Granaries

N

0   100 m
0   300 ft

PHASE 5 About AD 198–300 When the fort was reoccupied in the mid-2nd century, store buildings were turned into workshops, granaries were built and barracks, defences and gates were altered and refurbished. During the stable and peaceful 3rd century, the civilian settlement, or *vicus*, grew up around the fort and prospered. The plan shown here comes from the evidence of geophysical survey as the settlement has never been excavated.

1 The Rudge Cup, a bronze bowl, originally enamelled, found in Wiltshire with the names of forts on the western end of the Wall, including Banna – Birdoswald

2 Bronze arm-purse containing a hoard of Hadrianic silver coins, found in the rampart on the eastern side of the fort

3 Figure of one of the hooded deities, or *genii cucullati*. These mysterious native gods are found only in north and west Britain

century, the situation was probably little changed by the legalisation of the soldiers' families (see page 33). The presence of women and children in settlements and on the frontier generally is well known from the evidence of finds and inscriptions. At Birdoswald there are two tombstones of children and children's shoes have been found in the fort ditches. The two gold earrings found on site were probably worn by women.

Although a soldier's pay was much reduced by deductions for food, equipment and membership of a burial club to provide for his funeral, there would have been enough left for entertainment. Taverns, gambling dens and brothels would no doubt have been a feature of the settlement. Gaming was a popular pastime both inside and outside the fort. Three dice have been found in the fort workshop and stones scored with grids for board games with pottery counters are also a common find.

In other settlements, temples to a number of deities have been found, such as temples to Mithras at Carrawburgh and Housesteads, to Mars Thincsus at Housesteads, and to Atenociticus at Benwell. Mithraism was an eastern mystery religion, exclusive to initiates and with a large following in the army; in the worship of Mars Thincsus, we see a Roman god of war linked with a Germanic equivalent by Germanic troops; and Atenociticus, like Coventina at Carrawburgh, was a

British deity of a particular locality. It is likely that there was a similar mixture of religous practice at Birdoswald.

The bath-house of a fort was also usually situated in the settlement. The Birdoswald bath-house has not been found, though it may lie near the river.

The existence of the military community would have attracted traders, from pedlars selling trinkets to civilian merchants who held official contracts to supply the army with all the commodities it needed, such as pottery, hides, food and timber. Essential craftsmen such as blacksmiths, cobblers, weavers, and makers and repairers of metal goods are certain to have been present. These people would have been drawn by an economy fed by army pay in cash.

Outside the settlement, little or nothing is known of the local population. Across the north of Roman Britain, people seem to have lived as they did before the Roman occupation, unlike the civilian population in the south who occupied villas and towns on the Roman model. The main impact of the frontier on the local population was economic because of the demand for grain, meat and other essential commodities. These would have been supplied locally at a fixed price set by the army's commissariat, or acquired from the locals as part of the Roman taxation system. The demands of the army probably left little disposable income with which to acquire Roman comforts – if, indeed, the inclination to do so existed.

4 Gold and enamel earring in the shape of Hercules' club, a high-status object found on site
5 Bronze and enamel brooches and studs from Birdoswald
6 The enamelled bronze Moorlands Cup, found in 2004 in Staffordshire, with the names of the western Wall forts (and a person, Aelius Draco) on its rim

31

Above: A scene from Trajan's Column showing Roman auxiliaries with oval shields fighting Dacian tribesmen carrying the curved sword, or falx.
Below: Inscription flanked by a palm frond and a Dacian curved sword, recording the presence of the First Cohort of Dacians at Birdoswald

A COSMOPOLITAN SITE

People from all over the Empire are recorded on Hadrian's Wall. Pottery found to the south of Birdoswald was made in Frisian forms which shows the presence of people from the Netherlands. G Cossurtius Saturninus of Legio VI Victrix, who died at the fort, was born in North Africa. But there is most evidence for a connection with Dacia (modern Romania).

In the late 1st and early 2nd centuries, the Dacians, under their king, Decebalus, were implacable foes of Rome. In AD 85, the removal of a legion from Britain to the Dacian wars led to the abandonment of Scotland and the fall back to the line of Hadrian's Wall. The Emperor Trajan defeated the Dacians in two great campaigns in AD 101–2 and 105–6.

Once Dacia was made a Roman province, Dacians were recruited as auxiliary Roman troops. One cohort was probably sent to Britain as soon as it was formed. Inscriptions record that it built the Vallum of Hadrian's Wall, and under Hadrian they were stationed at Bewcastle. In the early 3rd century, the unit, known as *cohors I Aelia Dacorum miliaria* (the first cohort of Dacians, Hadrian's Own, 1,000 strong), moved to Birdoswald, where it was based for 200 years. It is named on a whole series of inscriptions.

Though in these later times numbers were probably made up with British recruits, the Dacian heritage was not forgotten. Two building inscriptions were decorated with the Dacian curved sword or falx – also shown as the enemy weapon on Trajan's Column in Rome. A tombstone from Birdoswald commemorates a child who was born and died here. He was called Decebalus, after the Dacian king and hero.

Roman Army Organisation

Hadrian's Wall was built by the three legions of Roman Britain (II Augusta, VI Victrix and XX Valeria Victrix). The legions were the citizen soldiers of Rome. A legion comprised about 5,000 men and was divided into 10 cohorts of six centuries each. By the time the Wall was built a century comprised some 80 men and the first cohort had five double-strength centuries. Legions also contained cavalry. They included many specialists, such as surveyors, architects and builders. The legionary equipment of Hadrian's day was distinctive, consisting of flexible segmented armour, javelins (*pilae*), a short sword (*gladius*), and a rectangular curved shield, or *scutum*.

The wall was manned and garrisoned by auxiliary troops. These units were raised in the provinces and generally did not serve in their native area. Unlike the legions, auxiliaries were not Roman citizens. Until AD 212, this privilege was granted after 25 years' service to the soldier and his descendants in perpetuity. In addition, they were given the right to marry, which was retrospective to recognise existing relationships. Auxiliary units consisted of cavalry (*alae*), and infantry (*cohortes*), of a nominal strength of either 500 or 1,000. There was also a mixed unit, the *cohortes equitatae*, a cohort consisting of part cavalry and part infantry.

Auxiliary troops were equipped with chainmail shirts, oval shields, long swords and spears. The distinction between the equipment of auxiliaries and legionaries blurred over time. Auxiliary infantry, like Birdoswald's *cohors I Aelia Dacorum*, were divided into centuries. At 1,000 strong, the Birdoswald unit would have comprised 10 centuries, each commanded by a centurion. Auxiliary units usually stayed in the province to which they were sent. The ethnic composition of a unit gradually changed through recruitment directly from the province in which it was stationed.

The commanders of auxiliary units were called prefects (for smaller units) or tribunes. These officers were members of the social rank known as the equestrian order which formed the imperial civil service. The command of auxiliary regiments was part of their career structure, which began with three periods of military service, each lasting three years. The commander was thus not a long-term member of the unit. He lived with his family and household in a large residence next to the fort headquarters.

The Roman Army included the legions, who built Hadrian's Wall, and the auxiliary troops from all over the empire, who occupied the forts

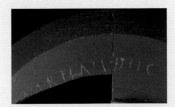

Top: Fragment of Samian ware cup inscribed 'Martini Diic' – Martinus the Decurion – a cavalry rank
Above: Auxiliary infantry of the Hadrianic period – with distinctive oval shields
Below: Roman spearhead from the fort ditch

END OF ROMAN BRITAIN

The last years of Roman Britain are obscure. Roman coins and pottery that could help date buildings cease to appear on archaeological sites because the system of supply, mass production and the economy had begun to break down. Written evidence for the period is incomplete and often contradicts itself.

During the closing years of the 4th century, troops were withdrawn from Britain as the Roman empire began to collapse. A number of British pretenders to Roman Imperial power, such as Magnus Maximus in AD 383 and Constantine III in AD 407, led armies from Britain to the Continent. These movements affected the field army, although not the frontier troops of the Wall, who seem to have stayed.

It has been suggested that there was a rejection of centralised Roman government in the province in AD 409, led by the provincial aristocracy, who objected to paying high taxes for an imperial defence and administration system that was no longer useful to them. The response to the end of Roman administration in Britain varied. At Wroxeter in Shropshire, Roman-style buildings were constructed in wood among the ruins of the old stone ones. These buildings, dated to the 5th and 6th centuries, show the continuation of a Roman way of life in some form. In the West Country, in the later 5th century, Iron Age hill forts were reoccupied as defence again became an important consideration for settlement.

'DARK AGE' BRITAIN

By the early 5th century, the Wall soldiers had been recruited locally for generations. For 90 years it had been compulsory for a soldier's son to follow his father into the army. It is not hard to imagine a military caste developing, with the command of a garrison being inherited from father to son.

When Roman administration in Britain ceased, so did the frontier troops' wages. Before AD 409 they had been paid from taxes on the local people. Some argue that they drifted away, but this seems unlikely, as it would have been an advantage to live in a fortified place. Discoveries at Birdoswald show that the 5th-century garrison did not leave.

The changes at this time in the area of the fort granaries provides evidence for the way these people adapted. The south granary, with its hearths at one end and the high-status finds dropped around them, is reminiscent of the halls characteristic of 'Dark Age' Britain. The two phases of timber building are almost certainly also halls and there are therefore three phases of such buildings on the site. This suggests that the late-Roman frontier troops gradually adopted a different social structure, perhaps evolving into a small war band, no longer dependent on a central authority but self-sufficient within a small area from which they could take supplies in

Above: Apart from these small penannular brooches made in bronze and iron, no other artefacts of the latest Roman phases have been found at Birdoswald

exchange for protection. Their base within the fort walls would have given them legitimacy as the heirs of Rome. They may have continued to carry Roman standards and to call themselves Roman soldiers. Their leader may even have retained a Roman title. They possibly resembled the war bands of the native Britons, with the hereditary commander's family becoming the ruling family and the commander more like a chief.

It is part of the archaeologist's job to form theories that can be tested by future work. The centuries after Rome are little understood and much remains to be discovered. The importance of the timber buildings at Birdoswald is that they are the first step towards understanding this period at Hadrian's Wall. Subsequent research may overturn these ideas, but at the moment they fit the facts that we have.

With the desertion of the second timber hall, whenever that was, the story of Birdoswald is broken. We have no more information until 1200, except for the intriguing discovery of an 8th-century Anglo-Saxon pin to the east of the fort.

BIRDOSWALD IN THE MIDDLE AGES

Throughout the Middle Ages Birdoswald (as it was now known – the origin of this name is obscure) formed a small part of the Barony of Gilsland. The first person to be associated with Birdoswald after the Romans is Walter Beivin, who held the property from the Barony for the payment of a mark in 1211. In 1200, he granted a 20-acre plot called Haythwait to Wetheral Priory, consisting of the land between Hadrian's Wall and the Vallum, to the west of the fort. He also granted land north of the Wall to Lanercost Priory in 1194–1220. Walter's nephew was called Radulpho de Birdoswald in one document; the use of 'Birdoswald' as a surname suggests that Ralph had a house on the site. In 1295, Birdoswald was held by John Gillett for one tenth of a knight's fee (the value of the feudal service as a fully armed knight of a tenant to his lord). The documents are then silent for a century. This is not surprising, as the area was subject to raids by the Scots throughout this time. In 1311, Robert the Bruce burned Gilsland and it was raided again in 1333 and 1345. In 1362, Naworth Castle, centre of the Barony of Gilsland, was said to be of little value, as it required frequent repair and was at constant peril from the Scots. The next reference is in 1425, when John Vaux is described as 'of Birdoswald'. In 1502, Rowland Vaux held Birdoswald for one seventh of a knight's fee. The tower house near the west gate of the fort may be associated with the Vauxs. The Roman gate may have been occupied together with the tower house, and there is little doubt that the farm buildings associated with this structure lay where the modern farm does, as a medieval hollow way led through the Roman gate and turned left into this area.

Above: Anglo-Saxon disc-headed pin, from the 8th century, found to the east of the fort
Below: The 8th-century cross shaft at Bewcastle, north of Birdoswald – one of the most significant pieces of Anglo-Saxon art in the north of Britain

Above: View of Naworth Castle – its 16th-century owner, 'Belted Will', had inscriptions from Birdoswald in his collection

REIVERS AT BIRDOSWALD

The 16th century was the age of the 'reivers', the border robbers and bandits who made cattle rustling and theft a major industry on both the Scottish and English sides. Clans joined in shifting alliances and feuds were common. Special Border laws and customs evolved in the area to deal with these troubles. By the last quarter of the 16th century, the Birdoswald farms were tenanted by members of the local Tweddle clan. Although no complaints against these men are recorded, they may well have been reivers in their own right. In 1588 Robert Tweddle complained twice to Lord Scrope, Warden of the English West March, that 'olde' Will Ellot, 'young' Will Ellot and 'lang' John Ellot had taken 30 head of cattle and oxen, a horse, a mare and household goods. The same month, the notorious Nixons and Ellots of Liddesdale, in Scotland, took cattle, oxen and horses. In 1590, the site was raided again, when a Peter Armstrong of Harlaw burned and cut up their doors, taking 40 cattle and oxen, 40 sheep and goods. The bastle houses at Birdoswald and in Milecastle 49 were typical of the type of defensive building constructed as protection from this sort of attack.

After James I became king in 1603, steps were taken to suppress the reivers. Rough justice was meted out by landowners such as William Howard, 1st Earl of Carlisle (known as Belted Will), owner of Naworth Castle from 1588. Feuding continued at least until 1599, when Thomas Carleton was shot in Gilsland.

FIRST ANTIQUARIANS

In this same year Birdoswald received its first known antiquarian visitor, Reginald Bainbrigg, a schoolmaster from Appleby. One can only admire his courage and dedication in travelling to the site during such violent times. He wrote: 'Frome Lanercost I followed the Wall all ruinated, til I came to Birdoswald, whiche doth seame to have bene some great towne by the great ruynes thereof. The inhabitants did shew me the plaice where the church stode, the inscriptions ther are either worn out by the tracte of tyme or by the clownishe and rude inhabitants defaced.'

The 'church' may have been the remains of the drill hall. In ruin, with its nave and aisles separated by columns, it would have looked much like the ruins of the dissolved abbeys. Bainbrigg saw inscriptions from Birdoswald at Naworth Castle, where they formed part of a collection formed by 'Belted Will' Howard. In 1603, Howard commissioned a survey of the Barony of Gilsland which recorded the bastle house at Birdoswald, the home of Thomas Tweddle, whom Bainbrigg had visited. Henry Tweddle also occupied a cottage within Milecastle 49, the remains of which are still visible. During the later 17th century, the Birdoswald bastle house was succeeded by a building which now forms the oldest part of Birdoswald farmhouse. Inside the porch is a 17th-century doorway. Only the eastern end of the house is this old.

By the mid-18th century, the tenant farmers of the Barony of Gilsland had become freeholders. Anthony and Margaret Bowman added the main part of the house in 1745, the year of the Jacobite Rebellion. Just before it was built, the great 18th-century Wall scholar John Horsley visited the site.

The Bowmans are buried in Lanercost churchyard. Anthony died in 1778 and was succeeded by his son William. William was visited in 1802 by William Hutton, an elderly man who made a walking tour along the Wall and published a book about his experiences. Hutton may have been the first to walk the Wall but he was certainly wrong in his belief that he would be the last. By 1830 the site was owned by Thomas Crawhall who was the first to undertake excavations and was at work when John Hodgson visited in 1833, collecting material for his *History of Northumberland*.

Above: Portrait of Sir Walter Scott (1771–1832) by Sir William Allan
Below: Gilsland Spa Hotel, built when the Newcastle-Carlisle railway brought visitors in large numbers for the first time to the Birdoswald area

WALTER SCOTT AND THE VICTORIANS

Gilsland was briefly a fashionable spa during the late-18th and early 19th centuries. Sir Walter Scott first visited in 1797 and became a regular visitor. He set part of his novel *Meg Merrilees* in the area. On one visit Scott met Charlotte Carpenter, his future wife, at the Spa Hotel and after a short time proposed by the river at the rock which became known as the 'Popping Stone' as it was here that he 'popped the question'. The rock is smaller now as the Victorians chipped off slivers of it as keepsakes.

Scott's own romantic vision of the borders may have influenced Henry Norman who bought Birdoswald in the 1840s. The landscape which Norman created at the site – classical ruins with sheep grazing over them and a mock

Above: Participants in the 1886 second Pilgrimage of Hadrian's Wall, with the great Wall historian John Collingwood Bruce (seated front right, wrapped in a shawl) at Lanercost Priory

medieval tower house – certainly fitted well with romantic taste. He built the Gothic-style porch and tower and laid out a garden over the site of the granaries, using the south wall of the south granary as a ha-ha to keep out the sheep in the fields beyond.

150 YEARS OF EXCAVATIONS

In the 1850s, the Potter brothers from Newcastle excavated the main south and east gates and the two minor gates and left the ruins exposed. Norman's son, Oswald, allowed the first scientific excavation at Birdoswald. Francis Haverfield and the Cumberland Excavation Committee were working on some of the major problems of the frontier and between 1895 and 1899 they worked on the newly discovered Turf Wall and the course of the Vallum in the Birdoswald area. In 1927, the celebrated Wall excavator F G Simpson decided to focus on Birdoswald, beginning seven important seasons of work, first by the Durham University Excavation Committee and then by the revived Cumberland Excavation Committee. Simpson was joined by two young archaeologists who were later to achieve prominence in Roman frontier studies as Professor Eric Birley and Professor Sir Ian Richmond. They excavated the spur to the south of the fort and discovered the Vallum crossing. The excavation of 1929 was the most important, as this was the first time that any fort interior was subject to stratigraphic excavation.

In the 1930s, the Birdoswald estate was sold to Lord Henley, who placed the walls and gates of the fort in state guardianship. In 1984, Cumbria County Council acquired the estate. From 1987, English Heritage carried out excavations and, in 2004, took over its management.

Memories of Birdoswald

We often found bones and bits of Roman pottery. I've still got an urn I turned up when ploughing, from AD 300

John Baxter, shown below as a young man, farmed at Birdoswald from 1956 to 1984

'My family has farmed around here for generations. We moved to Birdoswald in 1956 and were there for 28 years. It was a lovely spot: a big house and half an acre of lawn with shrubbery round it. We had no mains water. We pumped it from the river (it wouldn't pass today's safety tests). And we had a generator, not being put on the electric until 1965. There was only one toilet and that was outside. When the odd tourist asked to use the loo, if they were American, they'd refuse to use it.

'We often found bones and bits of Roman pottery. I've still got an urn I turned up when ploughing, from AD 300. Unfortunately, the plough went through it and broke the top. My youngest son found a Roman bead on top of a molehill.

'Some say there's a ghost – the Grey Lady – but I'd take that with a pinch of salt. The people who lived there before us reckoned they heard chairs falling over in the night. They say it has something to do with the statue of a goddess that was kept in a passageway and is now in Tullie House. But we never heard anything. Mind you, we'd tease the new hired hands. One man was so scared after a picture fell off the wall one night that he left the next morning.

'Back then, Birdoswald was a home, with hens and a collie dog running around, and livestock in the sheds. Now there's no noise and the swallows can't get into the barns to nest. That's sad.

'We took the place for granted. But since they've excavated and we've gone away, we've realised it is a big thing.'

Birdoswald's historic landscape

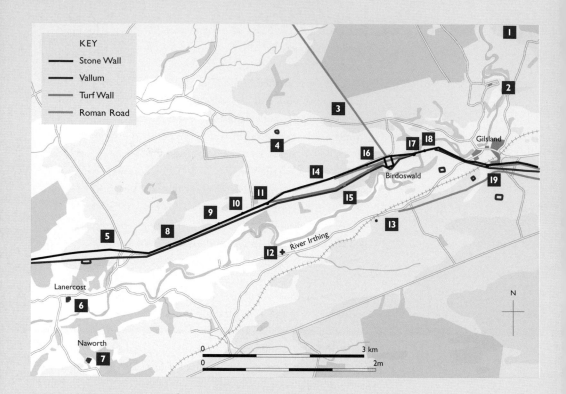

The area around Birdoswald is dominated by the remains of Roman frontier works. Stone structures are still visible, although the earthworks are harder to identify. The medieval landscape of castles and churches, all built out of stone quarried from the wall, reflect a turbulent frontier story.

AREA MAP

1 'Popping Stone' where Sir Walter Scott proposed to Charlotte Carpenter

2 Gilsland Spa Hotel – fashionable in Victorian times

3 Maiden Way

4 Castle of Triermain – in whose lordship Birdoswald once came (*not accessible to the public*)

5 Hadrian's Wall at Hare Hill, the highest surviving part of the Wall

6 Lanercost Priory

7 Naworth Castle (*not open to the public*)

8 Turret 52a

9 Turret 51b

10 Turret 51a

11 Vallum at Appletree (*not open to the public*)

12 Nether Denton Roman Fort

13 Roman Signal Station

14 Hadrian's stone wall

15 Site of Turf Wall, Milecastle 50

16 Turret 49b

17 Harrow's Scar Milecastle 49

18 Roman bridge, Willowford

19 Poltross Burn Milecastle 48